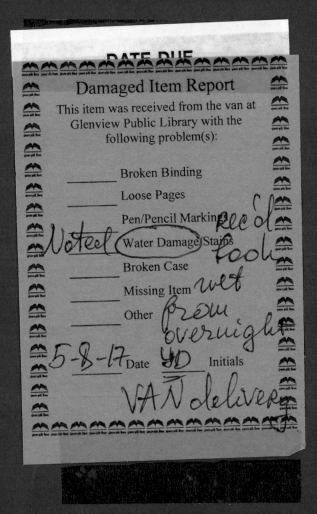

DATE DUE

Damaged Item Report

This item was received from the van at
Glenview Public Library with the
following problem(s):

_____ Broken Binding

_____ Loose Pages

_____ Pen/Pencil Markings

Noted (Water Damage/Stains) rec'd
took

_____ Broken Case

_____ Missing Item wet

_____ Other from
overnight

5-8-17 Date YD Initials

VAN delivery

Guess What Is Growing Inside This Egg

To Nathan

Guess What Is Growing Inside This Egg

Mia Posada

M Millbrook Press • Minneapolis

This egg sits snugly on its father's feet.
He warms it with his body's heat.

Under his feathered belly, it's cozy and warm,
Safe from the icy Antarctic storm.

Can you guess what is growing inside this egg?

A penguin!

This baby penguin, or chick, lives in Antarctica, one of the coldest, windiest places on Earth. When it is hatched, its mother returns from the sea to help care for it. Now its father needs to hunt for food. He hasn't eaten in the two months that he has cared for the egg! The mother and father penguins take turns holding the little chick on their feet to keep it warm, and going to the sea to hunt for fish and squid to feed it. Once it grows its waterproof feathers, the chick will be able to swim and hunt on its own.

Can you guess what is growing inside these eggs?

This mound of dirt and sticks piled high
Makes a safe nest for these eggs to lie.
Predators of the swamp had better keep back.
This sharp-toothed mother will attack!

Alligators!

These baby alligators will grow to be nine or more feet long. They spend most of their time in the swamp water, floating on the surface or diving below like a submarine. They use their long tails as paddles to push themselves through the water. They hunt for birds, turtles, snakes, and fish to eat. Alligators cannot chew their food. They grab their prey with their strong jaws and swallow it whole.

Tall lakeshore reeds help hide the nest
Where these eggs lie under their mother's breast.

Can you guess
what is growing
inside
these eggs?

Ducklings!

As soon as their feathers are dry, they will be able to follow their mother to the nearby lake. The brother and sister ducklings walk in a line, one after the other. Ducklings do not need swimming lessons—they are born already knowing how to swim. With their webbed feet, they paddle through the water. Soon they learn to feed on worms, water plants, and insects just below the water's surface.

Their mother crawled from sea to land
To bury these soft eggs in the sand.

Can you guess what is growing inside these eggs?

Sea turtles!

The tiny baby turtles hatch under the sand. They use their flippers to push themselves up to the surface of the beach. Leaving the nest at night, they must find their way to the water on their own. It is a dangerous journey as crabs and birds like to eat the tiny turtles. Once they have made it safely to the ocean, the baby turtles swim far out to sea and feed on small sea animals called plankton. As they grow, they begin to feed on larger things such as jelly-fish and seaweed. When the female sea turtles are grown, they will return to the beach to lay their own eggs.

This round sac of silk thread
is packed full of tiny eggs.
Their mother spun it
with her eight long legs.

Can you guess what is growing inside these eggs?

Spiders!

Hundreds of baby spiders, called spiderlings, hatch from their eggs inside the egg sac. Then they tear open the sac and crawl out. Like their mother, the spiderlings have eight legs. They also have eight eyes, but they do not see very well. Each spiderling must find a new home. It sends out a thread of silk from its body into the air and lets the wind catch it. The wind carries the tiny spiderling away until it lands in a new place where it will build its web. This is called parachuting. The spider's web traps insects for it to eat.

Can you guess
what is growing
inside these eggs?

Hidden in a rocky cave
Deep beneath the ocean waves,
Their mother wraps her long arms around
To keep these eggs safe and sound.

Octopuses!

You can actually see the baby octopuses inside their eggs! They are only about the size of a grain of rice when they hatch, but they are able to take care of themselves. The tiny octopuses float in the water, feeding on plankton. When they grow bigger, they use their eight arms, called tentacles, to catch crabs, fish, and clams. The octopuses hide from predators by changing their color to look just like the sand or rocks around them. The baby octopuses grow quickly. In about one or two years, they will be full grown.

Actual size of eggs

penguin

octopus

sea turtle

duck

spider

alligator

Inside a duck egg

Ducklings incubate, or grow inside their eggs, for 26 to 28 days.

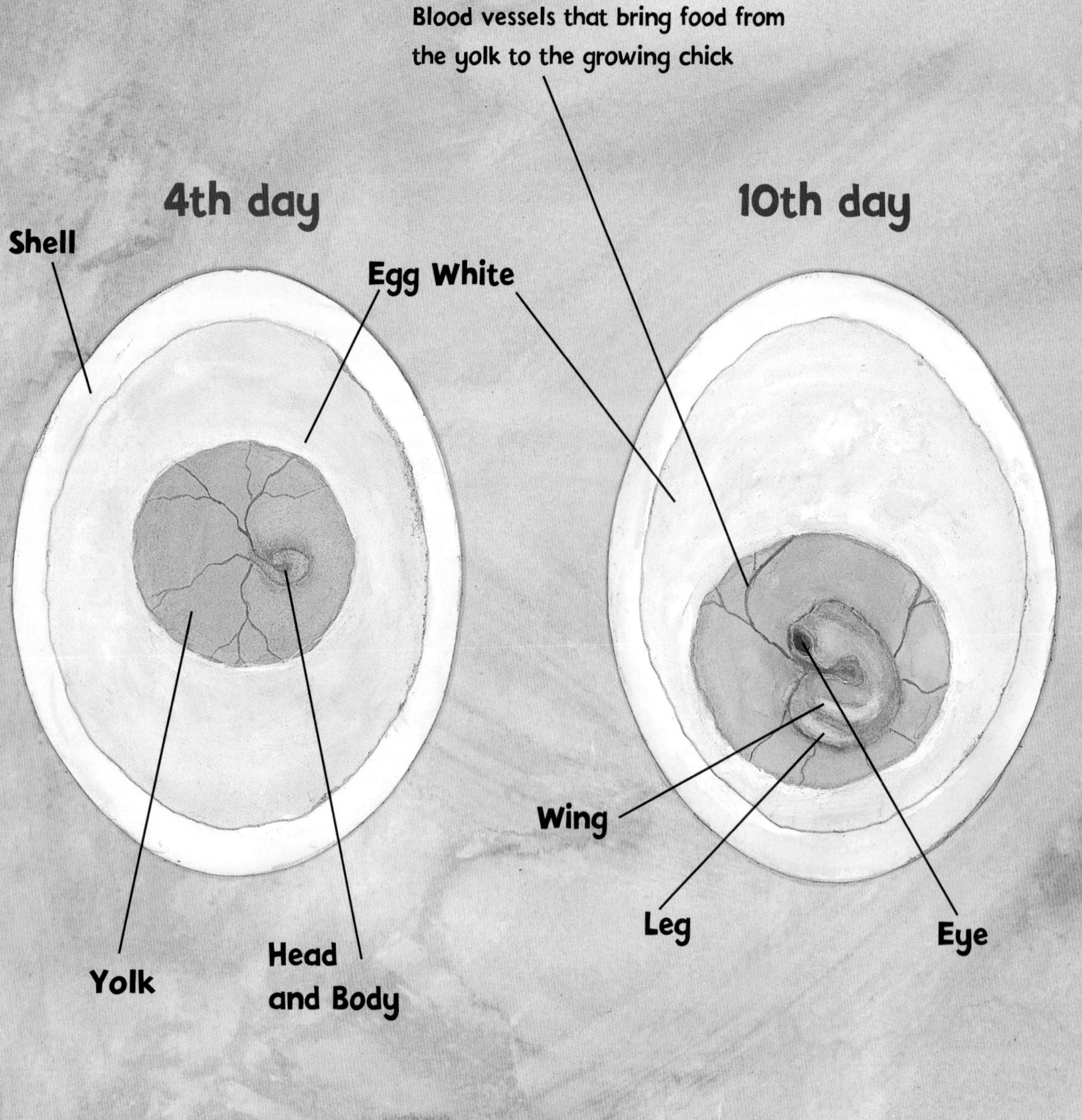

Blood vessels that bring food from the yolk to the growing chick

4th day

10th day

Shell

Egg White

Yolk

Head and Body

Wing

Leg

Eye

Incubation times for the other animals in the book:

Penguin: 2 months

Alligator: 2 months

Sea Turtle: 1.5 to 3 months

Spider: about 3 months (fall to spring)

Octopus: 1 month to 1 year depending on species

and temperature of the water (longer in cold water)

Egg tooth that helps chick break out of the shell. It falls off shortly after hatching.

14th day

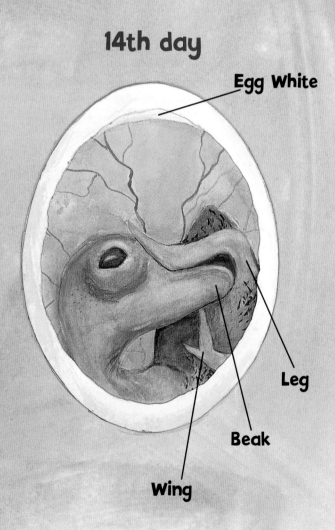

Egg White

Leg

Beak

Wing

26th day

Ready to hatch!

Millbrook Press, Inc.
A division of Lerner Publishing Group
241 First Avenue North
Minneapolis, MN 55401 U.S.A.

Website address: www.lernerbooks.com

Library of Congress Cataloging-in-Publication Data

Posada, Mia.
    Guess what is growing inside this egg / by Mia Posada.
      p. cm.
    ISBN-13: 978–0–8225–6192–7 (lib. bdg. : alk. paper)
    ISBN-10: 0–8225–6192–1 (lib. bdg. : alk. paper)
    1. Eggs—Juvenile literature. 2. Animals—Infancy—Juvenile literature. I. Title.
SF490.3.P67 2007
591.4'68–dc22   2006016250

Manufactured in the United States of America
1 2 3 4 5 6 – DP – 12 11 10 09 08 07